I Wish You Knew Me

Will's Story

Illustrated by Will Renken

Written and Edited by Mom (Marcy Renken)

Brought to you by

Showing Our Strengths Publications™

Copyright 2025

CONTENTS

1	I Know What You're Thinking	p 3
2	The Day Everything Changed	p 7
3	School Wasn't Made for Me	p 14
4	Finding My Passion	p 19
5	Becoming Independent	p 22
6	Future Plans—Kind Of	p 26
7	The Journey Continues	p 30

CHAPTER 1

I Know What You're Thinking

Why This Book Exists

I know what you're thinking, "A book? Really, a book? Why are you handing me this book to read that's all about you?"

Sometimes, I just can't find the right words to express what I'm feeling or thinking. Other times, I struggle to understand what people are trying to tell me. These challenges have been part of my life since I was a kid.

Learning to Explain Myself

Here's the thing. Sometimes I don't mean what I say. Sometimes, I say things I should not say. While I understand that it is pretty much never okay to treat people poorly or say things that aren't true or may come across as hurtful, there is some explanation for my behaviors.

Things I Struggle With

There are a couple of things I struggle with. One is that I struggle with my short-term memory. That means it is difficult for me to retain new information easily. It takes quite a bit more time for me to learn a new task than it would for an ordinary person.

Another thing I struggle with is that it is difficult for me to filter my thoughts before they become words. This is true especially when there is a tense situation, or when I am nervous or excited. I don't always have the ability to control what comes out of my mouth.

Sometimes, what you hear me say may be my original thought that I'm still processing, but for frustrating reasons my thoughts come out into words and can be hurtful to people around me. Just ask my brothers or my close friends or my parents.

Yeah, they've read this book too (or lived with me). They know my story.

CHAPTER 2

The Day Everything Changed

A Couch, an Exercise Ball, and a Bad Idea

When I was six years old, I was staying at a friend's house when my parents were out of town.

My friends and I were having fun jumping on a couch. We had the bright idea of using an exercise ball to bounce on, on top of the couch. The couch backed up to a railing that overlooked a 2-story foyer. I bounced off the ball and launched over the railing.

I fell 14 feet onto my head, onto the laminate-covered concrete entryway floor. That's when everything went blank for me for a while.

My mom usually picks up the story here although I don't really remember much about playing on the couch either.

A Day of Fun Turned Tragic

The firefighters, police officer, and paramedics, came to my rescue right away and took me to Riley Hospital for Children. I almost didn't make it to the hospital. There was a funeral procession and tour bus blocking the exit ramp for the hospital, and a delivery truck blocking the ER entrance. On the way to the hospital, I coded and had to be resuscitated.

The Miracle of Survival

I suffered from a severe traumatic brain injury.

I broke all three plates of my skull, although my head was the only thing I broke. It's a miracle that I am not paralyzed and there were no spinal cord injuries.

In fact, it's a miracle I'm even alive today.

Since I was a six-year-old, I didn't really want to stay in the coma and my body was trying to wake up. I think I was just trying to tell everyone I was OK.

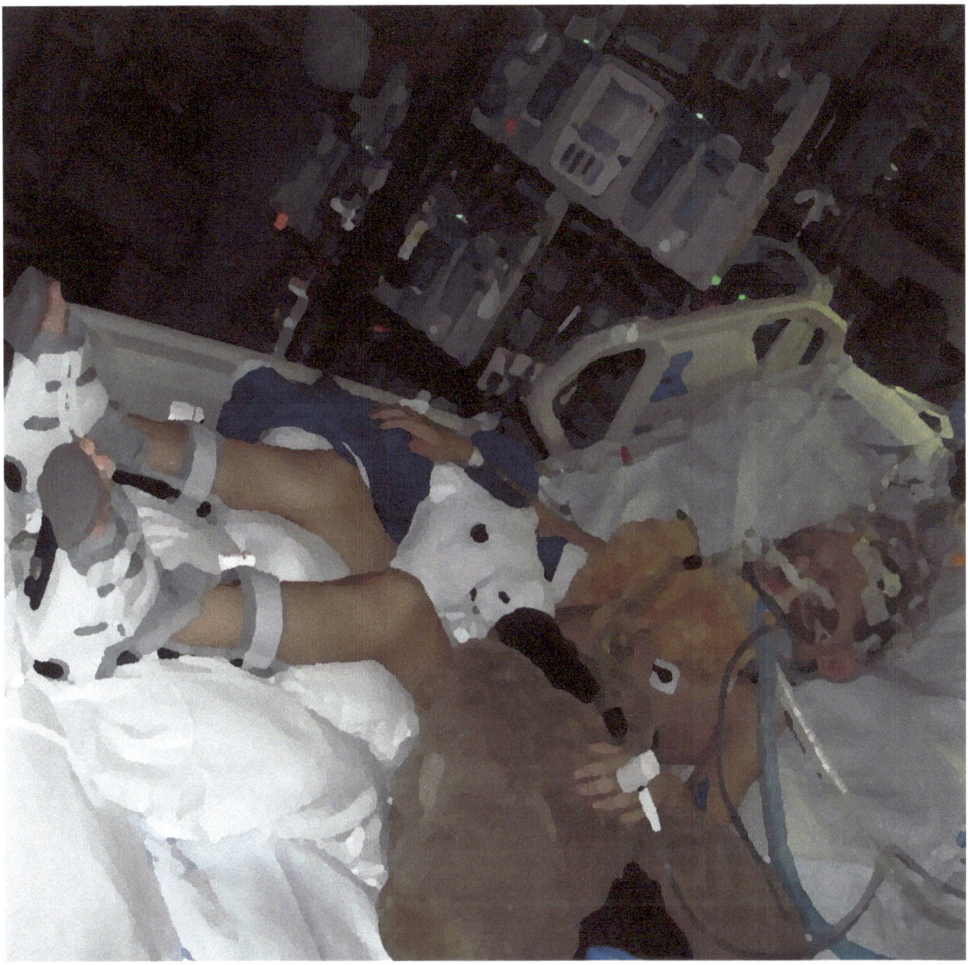

Scan me

Step Into the Story

13 Days in a Battle for Life

The doctors made a choice to put me into a coma. I was intubated, had a feeding tube, an art line, an ICP monitor, and an EVD drain to remove excess fluid. They said it would be a couple of days at most for the swelling to come down.

It ended up being 13 days before my brain stopped swelling enough to bring me out of the coma. That's when my long road to recovery began.

My parents said there were some scares while I was in the ICU. One day, I had fluid leaking from my nose. The nurse went out of the room to test it and when she came back she said,

> *"Well, we thought it was a problem, but it's snot. He has a runny nose!"*

The Long Road to Recovery

When they brought me out of the coma, my long road to recovery was just beginning.

Starting Over at 6

I had to relearn how to do everything all over again since I had been intubated, on a ventilator, and had a feeding tube.

It took a bit before I could even talk. I had to relearn how to eat, use my hands, how to write, and even how to stand and walk. It was a really strange experience.

My mom said it was like my brain hit a reset button. She said it was like I was a six-month-old in a six-year-old's body.

Facing the Unknown

We met several families at the hospital and even more people through sharing my story. The outcomes of other kids were not always the same as mine. Some kids even lost their lives due to complications in recovery from their injuries.

We also heard many stories of people who survived and went on to achieve great things.

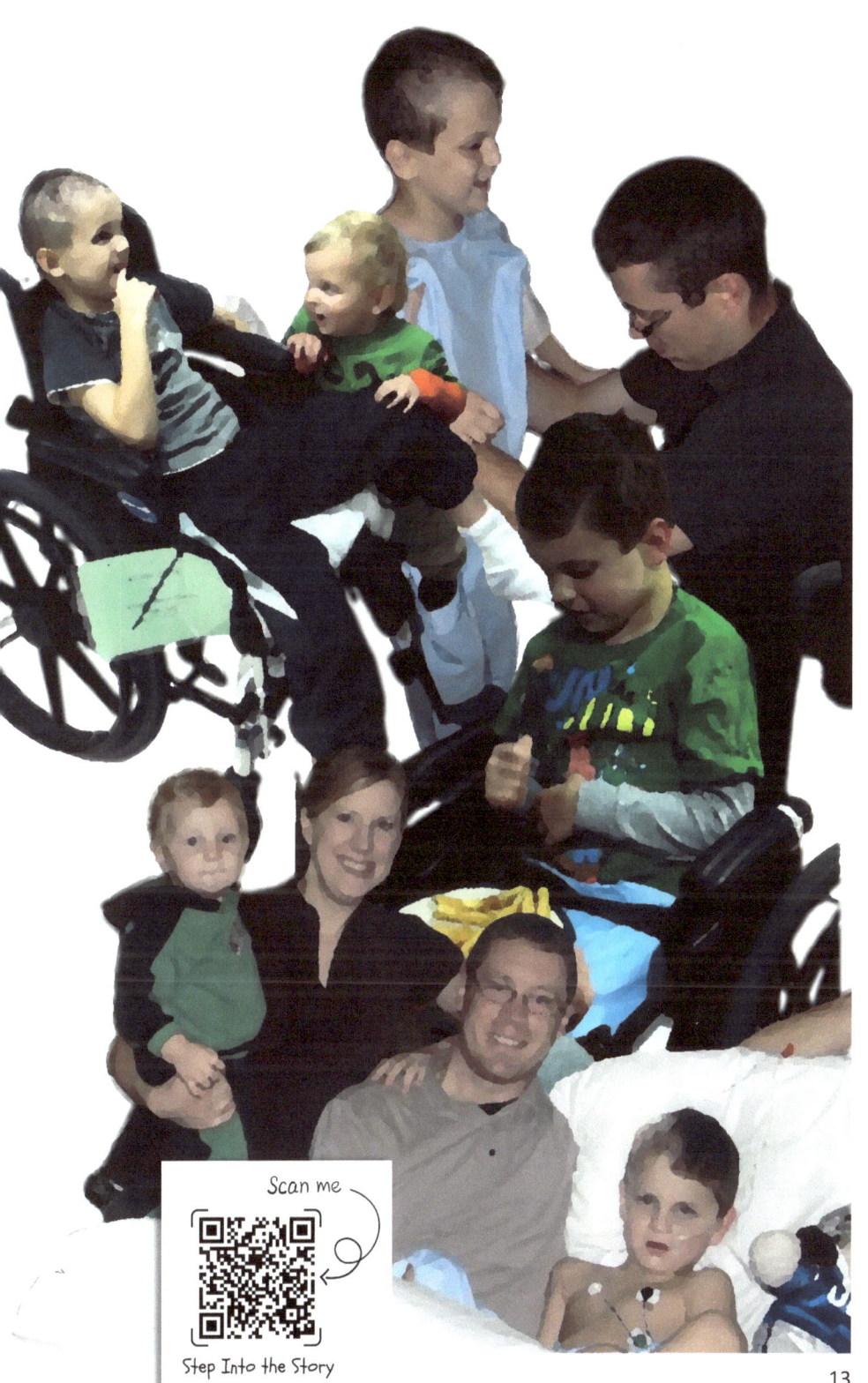

CHAPTER 3

School Wasn't Made for Me

Learning Takes Longer

I'm thankful I was able to relearn enough of the things I needed to do in order to fit in, to be a normal kid. But, being able to appear normal means my challenges are hidden. I have an invisible disability.

School was incredibly hard for me. It was hard for me to focus, to learn, to sit still or understand what people were telling me. Fidgeting seemed to help but no one wanted me to fidget either - unless I used those stupid fidget toys, which I did not like.

When Writing Feels Impossible

When it came to writing assignments, I struggled to get my thoughts written on paper. It usually came out scrambled. Or, the process

Will Renken

of writing would cause me to forget what I was even planning to write. That's still true today!

The doctors said any lasting effects from the brain injury would be known after two years. Because I was still young, they said the plasticity of the brain is amazing and I would be able to learn a lot of new skills –since my brain was still developing.

Lasting Effects and Support

At a young age, I had many people who were supporting me in different ways. I had a physical therapist, recreational therapist, occupational therapist, behavior therapist, resource teachers, aides, and doctors.

I always had new people coming and going in my life. Sometimes, it was difficult because I just wanted to work with one person. It seemed like right when I was making progress with one person, they would move on to another position. That only amplified how challenging school had been for me.

CHAPTER 4

Finding My Passion

The End of Soccer and Birth of New Interests

I played soccer when I was four years old until the accident. I really loved running and was pretty good at taking control of the ball while leaving the other kids in the dust. The first couple of years after my accident, I wasn't allowed to do sports. After those two years passed, I really didn't want to do sports even though my parents said I could.

Music or Art or Both?

When I was 8, I tried piano but I didn't have a lot of patience for it. I played trumpet for a few years but the idea of being in the high school marching band really scared me. I don't like being in front of people. I don't want to mess up.

I still liked music though.

When I was in high school, they offered piano classes, so I tried again. I really enjoyed it. I also got a guitar for Christmas when I was 19. I found a passion for creating new music.

Definitely Both!

I also found joy in creating art in high school. I tried ceramics for a year but was more drawn to 2-D art like sketching, chalk, and painting. Several pieces, that I completed in high school, are featured in this book. My art teacher, Mrs. Gullery, even gave me my high school diploma!

CHAPTER 5

Becoming Independent

A Constant Support

One person that has been with me through all these years, aside from my family, is my therapist. I've been seeing him for at least 10 years. He has helped me through a lot and has provided some great resources for my family to use in navigating the challenges that I face.

Mario Kart or Driving?

Learning how to drive has been a lot of fun – mostly. It has taken a while for me to really want to drive but learning how to drive - there's a challenge as well.

It Was Just a Bumper

I think I'm starting to figure it out. I haven't hit anything yet. Well, except maybe one curb. For

some reason, the bumper of my parents' car fell off when the front bumper scraped a curb.

The funny thing is, I was just backing out of our driveway! I'm getting the hang of it though. By the time you read this book, I will probably already have my license. Just like learning, tasks that have a lot of steps or processes take a while for me to get down.

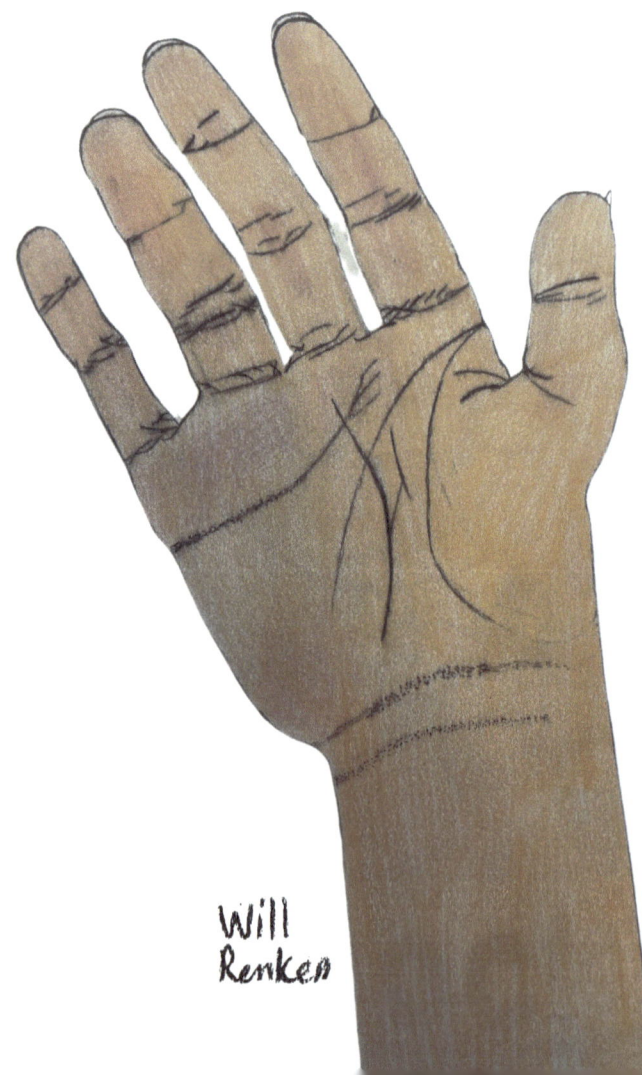

Will Renken

CHAPTER 6

Future Plans—Kind Of

College Aspirations

I will say I'm pretty proud of how far I've come. I know my mom is proud of me. She even started a whole business based on my story.

My next adventure is going to be college. I like the idea of pursuing art in a career, but I'm not quite sure what the career will look like. I'm working with a job coach who is guiding me.

Military Plans Changed to Art

For a while in high school, I wanted to join the Army. But at the time, the medication I was taking prevented it. My parents both served in the military and my uncle. Well actually, several uncles, an aunt, my grandpa, and some of my cousins too. I'm not sure that's what I want to do anymore.

I also like the idea of welding. I think it sounds cool to work with metal and make things people don't expect. There's an art school in Kentucky that I was accepted to! I would like to attend because they offer both art and welding! Who knows? By the time you read this, maybe I'll be there too or maybe I'll even have graduated.

Embracing Uncertainty

I'm not sure what my future holds but my mom always says God saved me for a reason so I'm always working to accept that.

The Amazing Renken Family

CHAPTER 7

The Journey Continues

I'm Doing My Best

If you've read this far, I thank you.

It's not always easy to share my story but most of the time it's nearly impossible because I can't quite explain it in the way my mom helped me to by creating this book. I just want you to know I'm trying to do my best. I think most of us are trying to do our best.

Encouraging Others Too

Part of doing our best is looking out for others. After reading this book, I hope you'll join in supporting me. Maybe you'll help guide me or coach me on my journey, even if just for a bit.

Then, maybe we can be an inspiration and a guide to others too.

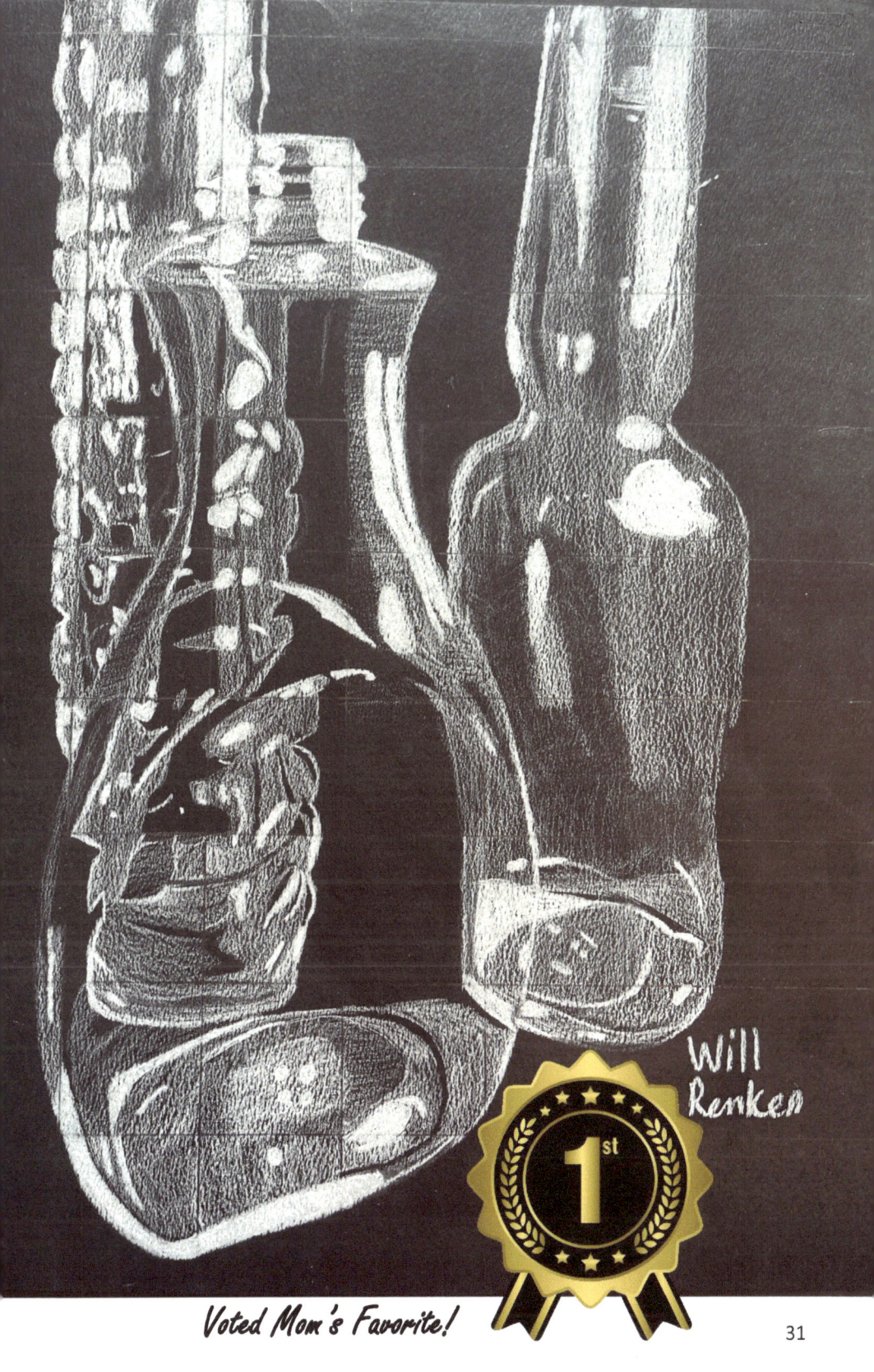

DAILY JOURNAL

Armory rooted in community
Modern facility preserves ancient oak

'HE WOKE UP'
After weeks in a coma following a fall, boy begins to heal

Youngster recovering from brain injury

An Autograph Page—Why not?

I Wish You Knew Me
Will's Story

Every life is a unique journey—shaped by experiences, resilience, and unseen challenges. I Wish You Knew Me™ books offer a meaningful way to share that story with others. Whether you're navigating a medical condition, a disability, a life transition, or simply want to be better understood, this book helps you express who you are with honesty and hope. It's a powerful tool for advocacy, connection, and awareness—written your way, in your voice.

Part of the Showing Our Strengths™ family, these books complement our children's Journey Books™, extending our mission of storytelling with purpose across all ages.

With compassion and clarity, we ensure your story is told in a way that empowers and inspires change.

When Life Gets Reel

Early on in this book, you'll find QR codes linking to videos that capture moments in my recovery journey. My mom thought it was important to include these in my book. Most of these videos were created by my aunt, Neti, while the final video, marking one year after the accident, was produced by my mom. Full web URLs are also provided below.

A Call for Prayers (Duration: 2:50)

 A heartfelt request for prayers just after the accident, when I was in the hospital.
https://www.youtube.com/watch?v=pFKrz-amB_E

Hospital Visit (Duration: 3:27)

 A glimpse of my hospital room during the coma, capturing moments of connection and hope.
https://www.youtube.com/watch?v=KJsAiLgKQO4

Messages of Strength (Duration: 4:35)

 Encouraging messages sent to my parents, Tom and Marcy, to encourage them and inspire others too.
https://www.youtube.com/watch?v=vIy6q2Dbi1Q

Witnessing a Miracle (Duration: 9:12)

 A nurse's response to my progress and moments that felt truly miraculous.
https://www.youtube.com/watch?v=e-3ElDZ9GM4

One Year Later (Duration: 2:50 minutes)

 A summary of the first year post-accident and progress I made.
https://www.youtube.com/watch?v=K5eInjLdr2s

Brought to you by

Contact Information

IWishYouKnewMe.org

I Wish You Knew Me™ for adults with special needs.

JourneyBookStories.com

Journey Books™ for children with special needs.

www.ingramcontent.com/pod-product-compliance
Lightning Source LLC
Chambersburg PA
CBHW041528090426
42736CB00036B/237